Contents

Your body

Your body is amazing.
It can do so many things.
Your body can move and grow.
Sometimes it can even fix itself
when something goes wrong.

Healthy Habits

by Kelly Gaffney

Engage Literacy is published in the UK by Raintree.
Raintree is an imprint of Capstone Global Library Limited, a company incorporated in England and Wales having its registered office at 264 Banbury Road, Oxford, OX2 7DY – Registered company number: 6695582

www.raintree.co.uk

Editorial credits
Carrie Sheely, editor; Cynthia Della-Rovere, designer; Eric Gohl, media researcher; Laura Manthe, premedia specialist

Image credits
Getty Images: Donald Iain Smith, 13 (bottom); iStockphoto: FatCamera, 14, 22, monkeybusinessimages, 13 (top), nycshooter, 9 (right), petrenkod, 17 (top), Wavebreakmedia, 10; Shutterstock: Africa Studio, 6 (right), Alexandr Makarov, 18 (left), Billion Photos, 18 (right), bitt24, 6 (middle), BY213, 24 (grumpy), DN1988, cover (shoe), Elena Schweitzer, 6 (middle left), elenabsl, 24 (exercise), Evdokimov Maxim, 6 (left), Fotokostic, 5, Friends Stock, 20, George W. Bailey, 7, Jeff Lueders, cover (clock), Khosro, 9 (left), Kim Reinick, 21 (bottom), KPG Payless2, 19, KRPD, 17 (bottom), margouillat photo, 6 (middle right), matsabe, 24 (machine), Maxim Vigilev, 24 (hour), Monkey Business Images, 1, 11, 23, Nattika, cover (food), pikepicture, 24 (schoolwork), Pressmaster, 15, Spreadthesign, 24 (heart), Suzanne Tucker, 4 (left), TinnaPong, back cover, 4 (right), valterZ, 24 (brain), Vertes Edmond Mihai, cover (ball), wavebreakmedia, cover (girl), 21 (top), WhiteDragon, 24 (sunscreen), Yeti Studio, cover (mask)

Printed and bound in China.

Healthy Habits
ISBN: 978 1 4747 9959 1

Your body is like a *machine*
that can do lots of different
things at once.
Machines need to be cared for
to work well.
And if you want your body to work well,
you need to care for it too!

Healthy eating

One way to care for your body
is to eat healthy food.
This can help you grow
and keep your body strong.

Try to eat lots of different foods
so that your body gets what it needs
to stay healthy.

You need to choose foods
from each of these groups:

| fruit | vegetables | meat, fish, eggs, nuts, seeds | dairy foods | grains |

Try not to eat foods
that have a lot of sugar
or salt in them.
Too much sugar and salt
is not good for you.

salt   sugar

Sometimes people can't eat some foods
because they can make them ill.
If you can't eat some of these foods,
there are other healthy foods
you can eat instead.

Did you know?

It is good to eat vegetables
of different colours. Every
colour has something
different that your body
needs to stay healthy!

Drink water

Your body needs water.
You should drink water every day.
If you don't drink enough water,
it can be harder to think.
You can start to feel *grumpy* or unhappy.

Drinking water also helps keep you cool.
Try to drink lots of water on hot days
and when you are playing sport
or running around.

Did you know?

Most of your *brain*
is made up of water.

Caring for your teeth

Healthy teeth are very important.
You need your teeth to bite
and chew your food.

You can take care of your teeth
by making sure you brush them
every morning and night.
Brush your teeth for at least two minutes.

Foods and drinks that have a lot of sugar in them are not good for your teeth. Try not to have them too much.

Sleep

Getting enough sleep helps you learn
and makes you feel happier.
Most children should try to get
between 9 and 12 *hours* of sleep
every night.

If you find it hard to fall asleep,
there are lots of things that you can do.
Make sure that your bedroom is quiet
and dark.

Your room shouldn't be cold or too hot.
Don't watch TV or have other screen time
before going to bed.
Do something quiet like reading a book.

Don't have screen
time right before bed.

You can use a night light if you
don't like it being too dark.

Exercise

If you want your body to be healthy,
you need to *exercise*.
Moving your body helps you stay strong,
and it keeps your *heart* healthy.
It can help you feel happier, too.

You should try to exercise
for at least one hour a day.
You can get exercise playing sport
or walking a dog.

You can also get exercise walking to school or riding your bike.

You don't have to do all your exercise at one time.
You can do it at different times of the day.

Did you know?

Exercise can help keep your bones strong, too!

Be safe in the sun

It's great to be outside in the sun
on a warm day.
But it is important to protect your skin.
Too much light from the sun
can be bad for your skin and eyes.

Try not to play in the sun
during the hottest part of the day.
Use *sunscreen* when you play outside.
A hat and sunglasses can protect you
from the sun, too.

Put on sunscreen before going outside.

Wash your hands

Washing your hands can
stop you from getting ill.
Always wash your hands
before you have something to eat.
You should also wash your hands
after going to the toilet
or blowing your nose.
Wash your hands after playing
with pets or playing outside, too.

When you wash your hands, use soap
and rub them together really well
for at least 20 seconds.
Just putting your hands under the water
won't get them clean.

Relax!

Sometimes your week can seem very busy.
You have to do *schoolwork*,
and you might play sport, too.
You might have to do things to help
around the house.

Make time every day to do something
that you enjoy.
Doing things that you enjoy
can help you relax.
You could play with your pet,
draw a picture
or read.

There are lots of things that you can do to care for your body.
Try to do these things every day.
Your body is like a machine.
Keep it working well!

Picture glossary

brain

heart

schoolwork

exercise

hour

sunscreen

grumpy

machine